C000046461

The Reconstruction of Ypres

The Reconstruction of Ypres

A walk from Cloth Hall to Menin Gate

Revised edition

Dominiek Dendooven
Jan Dewilde

Published in co-operation with In Flanders Fields Museum, Ieper

Uniform
an imprint of Unicorn Publishing Group
5 Newburgh Street, London
W1F 7RG
www.unicornpublishing.org

All rights reserved. No part of this publication may be reproduced, stored in a retrieval system or transmitted, in any form or by any means, electronic, mechanical, photocopying, recording or otherwise, without prior permission in writing from the publisher.

© Dominiek Dendooven, Jan Dewilde
This edition first published by Uniform, 2020
First published 1999

The majority of images in this guide are from the Paul Vandenbussche collection. He collected more than 5,000 of his hometown, mostly unique photographs, from before the First World War. In 2009 he donated his collection to the Municipal Museums of Ypres. This book is gratefully dedicated by the authors to this fellow lover and benefactor of our beautiful city.

All photographs are from the collections of In Flanders Fields Museum and Yper Museum, unless stated otherwise.

Contemporary photographs: Birger Stichelbaut.

A catalogue record for this book is available from the British Library.

ISBN (ENG) 978-1-913491-04-8
ISBN (NL) 978-1-913491-31-4

Designed by Matthew Wilson
Printed by FineTone Ltd

Contents

Bird's eye view over Ypres after its total destruction, 1919. (IWM)

Introduction

PRE-WAR YPRES[1]

Prior to 1914, Ypres was a thriving country town with an illustrious past. With its military riding academy and infantry barracks, it was a garrison town. The presence of many officers meant that a substantial group of Ypres citizens could adopt a comfortable – affluent

even – lifestyle. The town's outer-districts were dotted with numerous country houses, and the inner-city being home to large numbers of noble residents. The rest of the population survived on the back of the production of flax, lace, cotton and soap. Since there was virtually no mechanised industry, the town maintained its ancient structures, buildings, and open pastoral landscapes.

Ypres attracted many tourists, particularly to the Cloth Hall, the largest non-religious gothic building in all of Europe. An abiding memorial to the town's medieval hey-day and a monument that had survived centuries of periodic siege and war. The frescoes in the Cloth Hall, painted by Swerts, Guffens, Pauwels and Delbeke from 1861 to 1891, constituted an added attraction, portraying the town's grand past – or rather a romanticised view of it – in metre-high colourful scenes. The other historical buildings in the town also drew great interest, not only from tourists but also from (architectural) historians.

The municipal authorities were very conscious of the importance of the many monuments the town was rich in. At the end of the nineteenth century, a grandiose restoration programme was launched. In 1895, Jules Coomans – who had been backed by minister-to-be Joris Helleputte – was appointed city architect. Under his aegis, all the notable buildings wer surveyed and restored. By 1914, the works were as good as complete.

---

1   As the French spelling 'Ypres' is much better known in English than the contemporary Dutch spelling of the town 'Ieper', we use the former throughout this book. Throughout the ages the town's name has been spelled in many variations: Yperen, Ypern, Ypre, Ieperen and Yper are just some.

Panorama of pre-war Ypres with St Martin's Church, the Cloth Hall with Belfry, St James's Church, St Nicholas Church and St Peter's Church.

THE DEATH OF YPRES

On 4 August 1914, Belgium became involved in what was then still called the 'European War'. There was no reason to suppose that the sleepy tourist town of Ypres would become the symbol of the destructive power of modern warfare. Even during the first months of the war, the Westhoek – the western corner of Flanders – managed to escape the violence. But, in the autumn of 1914 there was a shift in the character of the war that would later be referred to as the Great War, and later still as the First World War – it had transitioned from a war of movement and fluid battlelines to a war of attrition, with both sides digging in. With the front running in one solid line from Nieuwpoort in Belgium to the border of Switzerland, Ypres was the last hole in the line to be plugged. For that reason, there was at

Ypres, a bulge in the line – a 'salient' to give it its proper military term. From mid-October 1914 until the end of September 1918, the medieval town was the focal point of the notorious Ypres Salient. During these four years, the front line was located just 11 kilometres away from the town centre at best and a mere 1.5 kilometres away at worst.

A German cavalry division entered Ypres on 7 October 1914, and left the following day with 8,000 loaves of bread, 62,000 francs from the city treasury and goods from plundered shops. The population was left behind, frightened but relatively unharmed in comparison with other Belgian cities. The First Battle of Ypres broke out two weeks later, sparing the town for now. However, from 18 November 1914, Ypres was systematically shelled by German artillery fire, with 10 to 20 shells falling every minute. Just days later, the most famous monuments of the town – the Cloth Hall and St Martin's Church – were ablaze. Over the following four years, the entire town centre would be wiped off the map.

In the first months of the war, like their city, many of the citizens of Ypres tried to survive the increasing hostilities – they took to their cellars or the casemates under the Vauban fortifications. Many died there, killed on the spot or fatally wounded. Of those who survived the shelling and bitter cold, hundreds succumbed to typhus. And yet there were still attempts to lead a daily life as normally as possible. Sometimes, even repair work was done to the damaged buildings.

On 22 April 1915, German troops used gas for the first time in history, to the north-east of the city. It was the start of the so-called Second Battle of Ypres. The Germans got to within a few kilometres of the city. A week and a half later, the last residents were forced to leave their shattered homes and businesses. After May 1915, there were only soldiers left in the town. On occasion, an individual was allowed in, under escort, to collect up a few belongings.

The gradual destruction of the city continued over the coming years. Although the front shifted a few

German cavalry in front of the Cloth Hall, 7 October 1914.

kilometres eastwards during the Third Battle of Ypres (July-November 1917), Ypres itself remained under constant artillery fire. During the German Spring offensive of 1918, the front line was less than two kilometres from the centre. By the Armistice, Ypres could hardly be called a town anymore.

In the winter of 1918–1919, a man on a horse was able to look right across the town. There remained just a few scattered houses more or less still upright. An example is the 18th century classicist Van der Mersch mansion designed by architect Thomas Gombert in Gustave de Stuersstraat: the house was largely protected by St Nicolas' Church standing to its east. The post office building too, a heavily restored medieval stone structure, was pretty much intact, as was the Biebuyck House in Diksmuidestraat. And by way of a miracle there even survived in d'Hondtstraat half a terrace of houses with a number of precious façades. But these were the rare exceptions to the general rule that no building in Ypres was built before 1920.

THE RETURN OF THE POPULATION

During the war, the whole population of Ypres fled or, from May 1915, was forcibly evacuated. Although, several weeks prior to the Armistice the first residents began returning home. Those willing to return found themselves living in a totally destroyed town where all but nothing remained. They used fragments of the debris and abandoned war material to build their first homes. But many were the previous residents who moved temporarily (or for good) to Poperinge, Kortrijk, Ghent, Bruges,

Australian engineers are making crosses for their fallen comrades in the post office building in Rijselstraat. (Australian War Memorial)

A view of Ypres from the ramparts, 1920–21. In the foreground a hut of the King Albert Fund. In the background we see the post office building in scaffolding. (IWM)

Brussels, or Ostend. Some of them would get together in their new home towns in Ypres clubs ('Cercles Yprois'). Alongside the 'Associations of the afflicted' they would campaign for a total reconstruction.

In the Spring of 1919, the Belgian government provided the first emergency housing in the 'Devastated Region' through the aid of the King Albert Fund. A few months later, the municipalities opened warehouses with provisions and building materials. A return on a grand scale only becomes possible through the 'comeback subsidy' (23 July 1919) and the promise of war indemnities.

Those who had the least to lose were the first to return, followed by those who stood to gain most from the reconstruction. Construction workers for example formed a quarter of the professional population in 1919. Those with private means of support and other well-to-do citizens stayed away from the chaos. Owners of previously large properties frequently sold their land and its demolished buildings. Nevertheless the town's population quickly increased: a town of just 6,000 inhabitants at the end of 1920, Ypres counted 15,300 inhabitants by 1930, or 90% of the pre-war figure. But the number of 'born and bred' Ypres inhabitants was limited: hardly half of all inhabitants had lived in the town before 1914.

SCENARIOS FOR THE RECONSTRUCTION

A variety of scenarios were envisaged for the town's reconstruction, many of which had already been drafted even while the war was still raging. British public opinion, with no less a spokesman than Secretary of State for War Winston Churchill, wanted to see the shattered Ypres preserved as 'Holy Ground': a symbol of the war and the British sacrifice. In direct contrast to this, was city architect Jules Coomans' plan to rebuild the city in its entirety, retaining a general 'Flemish, medieval and renaissance' appearance and precisely reconstructing the more significant historical buildings. From as early as 1916 he had burgomaster Colaert's support for this project. Of course, this ignored the opportunity to create a new city on the empty site, symbolising the modern age. Such modernistic ideas were given little or no prospect in Ypres.

When it became clear that the rapid return of the residents was making it impossible to preserve all the ruins, the British took solace in the preservation of a few of the more important ones. Brussels architect Eugène Dhuicque wanted to create a 'zone of silence' with the ruins of St Martin's Church, the Belfry and Cloth Hall, as a symbol of the irreversibility of history. What was lost, was lost: the Middle Ages had no more right to be commemorated than the war just over. On 14 July 1919, representatives of the British and Belgian governments decided to demarcate a 'zone of silence' in Ypres. The ruins of St Martin's Church, Belfry and Cloth Hall and the surrounding rows of houses would be preserved in a memorial park. A few days later, burgomaster Colaert registered searing protest. The owners of the surrounding houses stood up for their rights too.

Despite repeated exhortations from the British ambassador, under pressure from British public opinion, a definitive decision was postponed. Just two years later, the Britons relented,

abandoning their plans for good, and opted resolutely for the foundation of a grand national memorial: the Menin Gate. Meanwhile, the plans to build a modern garden estate on the borough surrounding Zaalhof and St Peter's Church were dropped. So now, nothing stood in the way of the reconstruction of historic Ypres, even though for many years support was still being voiced for preservation of some of the ruins.

THE FABRIC OF A (NEW) SOCIETY

As soon as enough residents had returned, many of the social activities revived too. Some pre-war societies reactivated, such as St Sebastian's (archery) Guild, the cultural society Davidfonds, or even the Ypres Union of Mutual Horse Insurance Societies. New groups were started up too, such as the Ypriana music band, the CS Yper sports association, the Puinentroost (literally: 'Ruins' Solace') theatre company and the war veterans associations. Individual recreational activities began to flourish, aided by the arrival of cinema. The 48–hour week introduced in 1921 meant more time for leisure activities. As soon as it became feasible, the numerous festivals and processions resumed. In 1919 there was a St Peter's Fair again,

'This is Holy Ground!' A warning sign in the rubble of St Martin's Church, 1919.

Start of the cycling race on the occasion of the St Peter's Parish Fair in front of the post office building in the Rijselstraat, July 1919.

in 1920 there were municipal festivals on 'Tuindag'[2] and a simple procession paraded through the streets. Another year later and the 'Cats Feast' resumed.

To return, all that was needed was a comeback subsidy, while temporary accommodation could be easily erected with war scrap. However socioeconomic recovery was essential for sustainable reconstruction. In mid-1919 when the great return was in full flow, it had become possible to find stocks of fundamental goods in Ypres. The provision of supplies was boosted by the town council's opening of a warehouse at the end of the year. Since production of goods and agricultural

products was pretty well non-existent, everything had to be imported. Despite rail transport's being dearer, the Ypres-Yser canal was never given priority and only became navigable again in 1933. The legendary Ypres-Comines canal was written off over the course of time.

The building industry was of course the most prominent in the initial years. In the beginning, almost everyone was occupied in clearing the rubble, constructing houses and levelling the fields beyond the city walls. People had to live on their own means until the government came up with payment for such operations. As soon as the decision for complete reconstruction had been settled, work began for real. A multitude of architects arrived – often from Brussels – and based themselves in Ypres for the coming years. Hundreds of labourers cleared away the rubble and sorted out which materials could be re-used. From 1921 – when the building lines had been set – the hordes of builders, bricklayers and carpenters

2 On 'Tuindag', 8 August, Ypres commemorates the end of the siege of the city in 1383, and honours its patron saint, Our Lady of Thuyne.

started on the process of building new houses and restoring the least damaged buildings per the architects' plans. The roads and utilities too were repaired by experts. By the 1930s, the reconstruction was for the most part complete and the challenge of finding appropriate work for townsfolk posed a new challenge for authorities. Local business initiatives lead to the founding – and re-founding – of semi-traditional firms such as breweries, diamond cutting and a few textile companies. None of these firms extended beyond purely local interest. Such development must await the growth of the Picanol loom factory in 1936. Real economic expansion of the city and district was only to follow in the 1960s.

In contrast to construction work, tourism was a lasting source of income. The moment the war was over, the 'Devasted Region' witnessed its first invasion of tourists. Every Belgian – and many other nationalities too – felt honour-bound to come and take a look at the now-legendary Ypres. The many ceremonies, inaugurations, and organised pilgrimages ensured that tourists would continue to find their way to the reconstructed town. In the 1920s, there was a veritable craze for monuments. 1927 saw the inauguration of the largest monument of all, the Menin Gate.

Public institutions reappeared as well. Local government and the police re-instituted themselves in a large hut on Minneplein in July 1919 and after a few years moved to the rebuilt Castellany Building on the Market Square. As a 'temporarilly adopted' municipality, Ypres had to pass many of its affairs over to the state, which was represented by a royal high commissioner whose office was in Surmont de Volsberghestraat. The

absence of the general building lines to appear and the financial burden – exacerbated by the cost of all the pre-1914 restoration work – were the greatest problems. The library started up in a hut on Minneplein too – relocating a few years in the barracks and then the state secondary school – being given a building of its own as late as 1933. In 1929, the Municipal Museum reopened in the rebuilt Meat Hall. The post office became operational again and in February 1923 could move into its reconstructed premises. Gas, water and electricity networks were restored, repaired and extended, as were the (local) railway lines. Ten years after the Armistice, it looked like the town had never been witness to any war. Practically all houses had been rebuilt – you had to look quite hard to find a gap in the municipal fabric.

Generally speaking, the reconstruction can be split up into two periods on an architectural level: the

— Porte de Menin
nockaerts: Première baraque réédifiée au milieu des ruines

Above: British soldiers and Belgian civilians on the terrace of 'In the New Telephone', a café, restaurant and shop near the Menin Gate, 1919.

Below: How reconstruction progressed in Ypres in the year 1920: by April 30 houses had been rebuilt, by December there were 461.

early- and late-1920s. The early 1920s (with the high point somewhere in 1923–1924) was when the majority of the houses were rebuilt in a very short period, and during which the town architect Jules Coomans was particularly influential. In a second period from 1924 until well in the 1930s, larger buildings and public institutions were completed. Here the architects could take a more creative approach with the remaining tasks. The unveiling of the rebuilt Belfry in 1934 may be considered as the completion of the reconstruction. There were only a few large public buildings covered in scaffolding, a situation that remained unchanged for years.

During the Second World War Ypres was little damaged, but the remaining reconstruction works were delayed. The wing of the Cloth Hall which now houses the Yper Museum was only put into official service as the Town Hall in 1967. And as late as 1990, the restoration of the Ypres ramparts was still being partially financed by war-damage compensation!

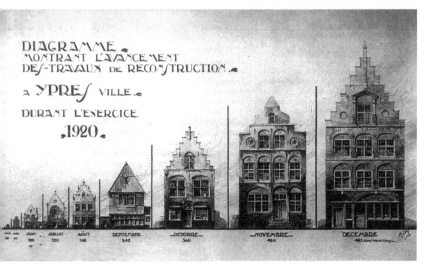

DIAGRAMME MONTRANT L'AVANCEMENT DES TRAVAUX DE RECONSTRUCTION A YPRES VILLE DURANT L'EXERCICE 1920.

A pre-war Saturday market in front of the Cloth Hall.

The Walk

I Belfry and Cloth Hall

This complex offers a unique and extensive administrative history; ranging from its architectural roots in the Middle Ages, to its cultural and identity-defining significance in the community today. Historically it served as the economic

YPRES, LA GRAND' PLACE

centre of the town, combining the Belfry, Cloth Hall and Town Hall. Today the building houses the In Flanders Fields and Yper Museums. Its stature as a huge civil architectural achievement from the Middle Ages cannot be understated. The side on Grote Markt is no less than 132 metres long. Belfry and Hall date originally from the 13th century. The 'Nieuwerck' on the east side dates from 1622. This graceful building above a gallery was built during a transition from late Gothic to Renaissance architecture, with early Baroque elements.

The reconstructed Cloth Hall is the outstanding symbol of the town arising like a phoenix from its own ashes after the First World War. On the wall right of the Donkerpoort – as the entrance in the middle under the Belfry is called – you can just about make out the point up to which the building was destroyed. Several stones in the wall still bear scars of the war, caused by the impact of exploding shells. Above the gate we see the statue of Our Lady of Thuyne, patroness of Ypres. On the right we see Count Baldwin IX of Flanders and Mary of Champagne, under whose leadership the construction of the Cloth Hall first went ahead, and on the left the Royal couple of Belgium during the reconstruction, Albert I and Elisabeth. The Donkerpoort is the element that has best retained its medieval character. Up until the destruction of the First World War, this Donkerpoort or 'Dark Gate' would have been considerably darker,

Above: The pre-war façade of the northeastern wing of the Cloth Hall looked completely different before the war, and was only rebuilt similar to the other wings after the Second World War.

because in the middle the 'Chamber of the Council of XXVII' was built against it, yet this room was not reconstructed. Under the Donkerpoort we can still see original sculpted consoles: little crouching figures bearing the vaulting on their backs. Through the courtyards, a visit can be made to both the Yper Museum and the In Flanders Fields Museum and museum café.

When we reach Sint-Maartensplein, we see on our right the eastern wing of the Cloth Hall complex. This wing, which is used by the Yper Museum, was only finished in 1967. It was designed by architect Pauwels in the style of the rest of the Cloth Hall. Before the war, there was a sober building here in a completely different style.

On 22 November 1914, the complex went up in flames, and at the end of the First World War, there remained only a part of the Belfry and a few blackened walls. The debate was already raging about whether to rebuild the Hall or not before the war was over. The town administration finally prevailed and from 1928 onwards the reconstruction of this monument was undertaken under the leadership of town architect Jules Coomans.

Above: The 'Chamber of the Council of XXVII' was built against the Donkerpoort but would not be rebuilt after the war.

Left: Jules Coomans, town architect of Ypres.

JULES COOMANS

Training, passion, religious zeal, and neo-Gothic fundamentalism are all aspects found in equal measure in the character of Jules Coomans, to whom the town of Ypres is greatly indebted for its reconstruction and architectural tradition. Coomans was born in Scheldewindeke (East Flanders) on 17 May 1871. He attended school at the Sint-Amandscollege in Ghent. In the adjoining Saint Luke's School, his uncle Frans Coomans (brother Matthias FSC) and guardian of Jules provided him with an artistic education.

At the age of 16, he was admitted to the University of Louvain for training as engineer and architect. Here, he became the apprentice and pupil of Joris Helleputte

who would later become a minister in the Belgian government. With the latter's support, Coomans was appointed town architect of Ypres in 1895. The restoration of Ypres' heritage was his foremost task, which was all but wiped out by 1914. During the war, he lived in Wimereux, near Boulogne-sur-Mer. While many archival records were destroyed during the war, he had been able to flee to safety with his plans and measurements of Ypres. While war was raging back home, he attempted, along with burgomaster Colaert, to propagate his ideas for the historical reconstruction of the town among a wider circle. Finally their ideas prevailed. Jules Coomans died in 1937. At that moment, St Martin's Church, the Belfry, and a part of the Cloth Hall had been completed. For the further reconstruction of the Cloth Hall, he was succeeded by P.A. Pauwels, who applied a stricter archaeological vision, in tune with the spirit of the times.

2 St Martin's Church

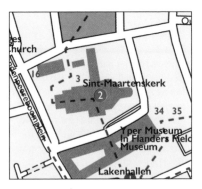

Enter the church through the south portal, continue along the ambulatory through the nave, leaving the church through the main entrance (west portal) under the tower.

The reconstruction of St Martin's Church also took place under the leadership of town architect Jules Coomans, who set about his work in a very historicizing manner. Before the First World War, Ypres' foremost place of worship had a truncated steeple, but in 1914 work had already started on a pointed one. During the reconstruction, completed by 1930, the pre-war intention was realised. An item that did not enjoy reconstruction is the Dean's Chapel dating from 1623–1629. This chapel adjoined the Church and was located

The ruins of St Martin's Church, 1918.

THE EVENTFUL HISTORY OF ST MARTIN'S CHURCH

It is presumed that there was already a small church or chapel in the 11th century at the location of today's St Martin's Church. During the course of the 13th and 14th century, it received a Gothic appearance. In 1433 the tower collapsed, but a few years later was rebuilt by Maarten Uutenhove from Mechelen. In 1465 the tower was complete, except for a missing spire.

During the Counter Reformation in 1559, 14 new bishoprics were set up. Ypres too became a Bishopric and St Martin's Church was elevated to the status of cathedral. For this reason, a Dean's Chapel was added. The most famous Ypres bishop is Cornelius Jansenius, who died of the plague in 1638. His posthumously published book 'Augustinus' caused a Catholic reformation movement to arise called Jansenism, which was condemned by the church as heresy. During the French

occupation in 1799, St Martin's Church was sold and in 1801 the bishopric of Ypres was definitively abolished. From the second half of the 19th century onwards, the Church underwent one restoration after another. Before the last phase was complete – the construction of the steeple – the Church went up in flames on 22 November 1914. At the end of the war, there remained nothing more of St Martin's Church than a pile of rubble. The main church of Ypres was, however, very close to town architect Coomans' heart and reconstruction work was started as early as 1922. In just eight years' time the job was done, and the Church, sporting a 100-metre steeple, was inaugurated on 15 July 1930.

Saint Martin's Church's South Portal with the never to be rebuilt Dean's Chapel to the left, before 1914. Also notice the church's truncated spire.

Left: Saint Martin's Church in full reconstruction, 3 February 1926.

on the present grassed area west of the south portal.

When we enter the Church through the south portal, we see to the right of the entrance door a memorial plaque for the French soldiers who fell in and around Ypres. The interior of the church has had a hypercorrect reconstruction. The tombs in the choir are original – they could be saved, being buried under the rubble. However, the memorial tablets for count Robert of Bethune and Bishop Jansenius are new. In the north transept, under the organ, you see a memorial plaque for the fallen soldiers from the British Empire. It is quite a sobering thought when you consider that this plaque commemorates a million dead, while other tombstones in the church were constructed for one single person. In the north-western corner of the nave is the baptistery. The barrier was made from fragments of the pre-war choir pews (wood), while the statues are from the pre-war barrier between church and Dean's Chapel. Often art treasures saved during the First World War are on display in the church, as well as photographs of the destruction and reconstruction. The church may be exited via the main (western) portal.

3 The Lapidarium

The so-called 'Lapidarium' is one of the few remaining ruins in the town centre. Until the First World War, this was the location of St Martin's Monastery which adjoined St Martin's Church. Part of the cloister survived the war, and is original. Jules Coomans

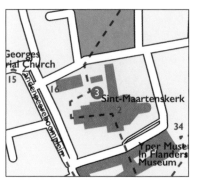

THE BISHOP'S GARDEN – PUBLIC GARDEN

What is now called Astrid Park was formerly the bishop's garden and, after the French Revolution, the Public Garden. The non-reconstruction of the Bishop's Palace used before the war as a courthouse complicated the present layout. On the left of the park, in Deken Debrouwerstraat, there is a natural stone pillar with a sculpture of Our Lady. Originally the pillar was part of a classicist pump on the corner of Boomgaardstraat and transferred to the site of the former 'Monastery Square' which was located here and not reconstructed. The pillar is a rare example of street furniture in the town centre to have survived the First World War.

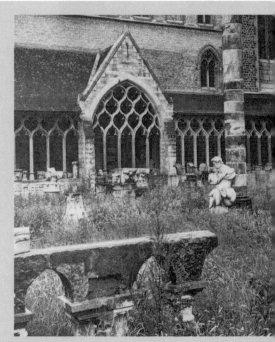

planned the reconstruction of the whole monastery, but his plans were never carried out, probably due to his death in 1937. The only part of his plans to see the light of day was the lengthening of the north transept.

On the façade, the interruptions in the merlons and other bricks, let you see clearly where the so-called Jansenius wing should have been built. Surviving sculptures and fragments in the former monastery garden today bear witness to the destruction during the First World War.

Left: The cloister of St Martin's Monastery during the war. The so-called Jansenius wing is almost completely destroyed. In the background we see a part of the ruin of the pre-war courthouse and behind it the trees of the 'Public Garden'. (IWM)

Above: A corner of Ypres that once stood here and has completely disappeared: the former bishop's palace, then in use as courthouse, with on the left the city library and on the far left the entrance to Kloosterplaats (Monastery Square).

Left: The Lapidarium in better times.

4

Surmont de Volsberghestraat 13: Froidure House

This imposing house was built around 1931. The house may well have been designed by the owner Edouard Froidure, better known as 'Bulte' (Hunchback) Froidure. The main façade along Deken Delaerestraat was inspired by the 18th century courtyard façade of the Malou mansion that was located in Sint-Jacobsstraat up to the First World War. The sculpture work on this house, among other things the flower and fruit garlands above the windows, was by the Ypres sculptor Maurice Deraedt, who will crop up many times in this guide. The owner of this house, Edouard 'Bulte' Froidure, had a great devotion to Our Lady, patron saint of Ypres, and expressed this admiration in this façade:

the sculpture of Mary and the medallion with the initials MR. Froidure, whose son was a priest, fervently hoped that Ypres would once again become the seat of a bishopric, as it was before the French Revolution. This house could then become the bishop's residence.

The facade of Edouard Froidure's house is based on the 18th-century courtyard facade of the Malou mansion, which stood in Sint-Jacobsstraat until 1914, but was never rebuilt.

EDOUARD 'BULTE' FROIDURE

Edouard Froidure, who commissioned the construction of this house, was one of the most remarkable inhabitants of Ypres of the late-19th century. This philologist and amateur astronomer was born in Ypres on 21 May 1864. He grew up partially in France, where he also married. The wealthy Froidure – he possessed several houses in Ypres – was an eccentric, but extremely pious figure. His house at number 22, Grote Markt, built in 1927, was dedicated to Mary and has a façade-wide loggia. From here, the future bishop of Ypres would be able to bless the population – or so he hoped. This prominent personality died on 3 March 1939.

5 Surmont de Volsberghestraat 20

This house on then Nieuwe Houtmarkt was called 'Au Jardin Public' before the First World War. To judge by the wall anchors, it was built in 1679. In 1922, it was rebuilt by the Brussels architect F. Verheyen in the so-called 'reconstruction style'. The year indications engraved in the stones of the entablement mention the three most important years from the history of this house: 1679 (construction), 1914 (destruction) and 1922 (reconstruction). The alley next to the house led, before the Great War, to the non-reconstructed St Christina Beguinage.

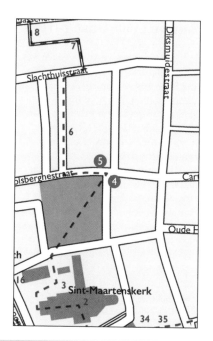

THE 'RECONSTRUCTION STYLE'

The eclectic architectural style respected by Coomans and his colleagues is based on a so-called architectural tradition which mainly reaches back to regional Gothic and Renaissance influences. Neo-Gothic delivers the principles: respect of tradition, attention to detail, and precise considerations of verticalism and horizontalism. The visible construction characteristics of the so-called 'reconstruction style' are the use of yellow bricks, occasionally accentuated with red brick, stepped gables decorated with tabernacle windows, decoratively finished tympanums, wrought iron wall anchors, etc.

'Au Jardin Public' inn, seen from the entrance gate to the 'Public Garden', before 1914.

6 Blauwe Leliestraat 2–16

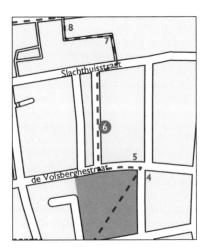

In the main streets of Ypres, space was allocated primarily to public buildings and large private residences during reconstruction. The houses that the workers would have lived in are instead to be found in the little alleys located more on the periphery of the town centre, as seen here.

The front gardens of these houses betray a certain influence of the garden city movement. Through the use of contrasting yellow bricks, every building layer is accentuated. These little houses were built in 'Flemish bond', that is to say, a bricklaying method whereby the rows of bricks are alternately laid with the long and the short sides abutting. During the reconstruction of Ypres, 'Flemish bond' was used extensively. Since the introduction of the cavity wall, this bricklaying technique has all but disappeared. The very fact that the technique is called 'Flemish bond' reflects how often the style was applied in Flanders.

THE ST CHRISTINA BEGUINAGE

Before the First World War to the east of Blauwe Leliestraat one could find the St Christina Beguinage. Originally it was located outside the town walls, but after the siege of 1383 it was transferred here.

The beguinage consisted of two rows of houses set around an interior courtyard with the beguinage chapel located centrally. Most buildings dated from 1636. In 1787, a large number of the buildings were deserted and purchased by the town. Later, the Civil Almshouse authority converted it into an old people's home. From 1865 to 1914 the former beguinage was in service as a state police barracks. The horses' stables were located in the chapel. After the First World War it was not reconstructed.

The former St Christina's Beguinage.

Bird's eye view of the new park in 1931, with on the right the Froidure House under construction and the former inn 'Au Jardin Public'. On the large empty plain behind it was the Saint Christina's Beguinage until 1914. The houses in Blauwe Leliestraat of which we see the entrance on the left are not yet built.

7 Slachthuisstraat 20: The Little Hut

In the nameless street between Slachthuisstraat 18 and 22 is an exceptional witness to the solution of the housing shortage after the First World War: an authentic emergency dwelling. In contrast to the wooden huts provided by the King Albert Fund, this is a 'frame and brick' hut: a wooden structural skeleton with brick walls. Since its construction the then emergency dwelling has been modified and plastered many times. This dwelling, which is still inhabited, is a reminder that the 'semi-permanent dwellings' often out-survived their original intention. In the reconstruction years, most emergency dwellings had to be built at least eight metres from the building

The little hut in 2000, when it was already 80 years old.

THE KING ALBERT FUND

The foundation of the King Albert Fund (KAF) in September 1916, was the result of the Belgian government anticipating the housing shortage that would arise as soon as the inhabitants of the devastated regions would return. The foundation started up in 1917 with houses that could be dismantled easily and were designed with sides of 4 or 6 metres. But it was only in February 1919 that the KAF was allocated government subsidies and building could actually begin. However, the KAF was never able to meet all the demands: in the Westhoek of Flanders there were 1,924 huts available in February 1920 on a total of 7,721 requests. So people were encouraged to build their own homes in durable materials by means of a subsidy of 3,000 francs in the form of building materials. As for the wooden structural frame concept, it was met with little success.

Design drawing of a standard model KAF hut. (Belgian State Archives)

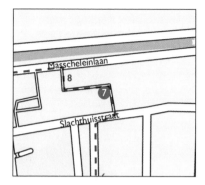

line. In this way the construction of the definitive houses on the building line would not be encumbered. That is the reason why the Little Hut is located in the middle of the block of houses. This hut dates from 1919.

Top right: The little hut in 2020.

Right: The entrance to the nameless street where one can find the little hut.

On 5 January 1925, the KAF was wound up by the government, as its task was considered complete. The government wanted to sell the huts, although they were almost all still occupied due to the relatively low rental. To prevent large numbers of people being evicted, the municipalities were obliged to purchase the huts themselves: in Ypres some 314 were bought. Thanks to repairs and modifications, many emergency dwellings remained in service for far longer than had ever been anticipated. These days, there remain about ten of these huts in the former front region.

8 Adj. Masscheleinlaan 21–25, 27–29

The low row of workers' houses located on Adjudant Masscheleinlaan 21–25 dates from the start of the 1920s. The architectural style of this terrace can be traced to the 'regional' tradition of brick building. With their jutting roof edges, interspersed with raised-top roof windows, these little houses are nothing if not picturesque.

The two little houses on the other side of the alley (Adj. Masscheleinlaan 27 and 29) are two semi-permanent dwellings. Along with the little hut in the street with no name, they form something of an exception in the town centre. Here too, the construction is wooden frame with brick walls, although now also hidden behind the cement surface.

LAGE WIELTJESGRACHT

Lage Wieltjesgracht, along with Hoge Wieltjesgracht to its east, gives an indication of the location of the innermost northern town ramparts in Ypres. The structures located here were demolished in 1853–1855. With the exception of the north-east corner and these northern 'grachten' or canals, the town of Ypres has kept its town walls reasonably intact. Both of today's canals are a vestige of the 19th century provisions for fare collection and drainage in Ypres. The name 'Wieltjesgracht' means 'Wheel Canal': probably a reference to the vertically mounted wheels of the lock that regulated the water level in former times.

Lage Wieltjegracht before the First World War.

9 | Veemarkt 9–11

The former guild halls of the boatswains (number 9) and the merchants (number 11) were 'approximated' during the reconstruction following the First World War. The original houses were built in the local renaissance style and dated from 1629 and 1623 respectively. During the reconstruction, the overall appearance of both houses was taken into account, but the execution is far less detailed than it was for the pre-war buildings. The boatswains' hall had a slightly lower plinth for example, and

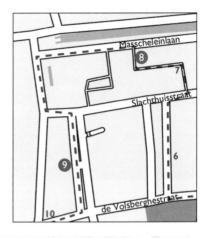

The guild houses before 1914.

the windows were not so high. But both houses did regain the relief work (a sculpting practice where the sculpture remains attached to the background of its same material) that they had exhibited before the Great War: on the boatswains' hall we see two ships, and on the merchants' hall we see on the left a representation of the money exchange and on the right a depiction of Mercury, the god of trade.

Before the war, there was a late Gothic stepped gable from 1544 on the right of the two guild halls. Until the late 20th century, this plot of land was empty. Since, the plot has been occupied by a new building that only vaguely recalls the pre-war situation.

VEEMARKT

Until 1686 the Yperlee flowed on the current location of this square. The Yperlee was the canalised river that brought so much prosperity to Ypres. This is the reason why the guild halls of the boatswains and merchants are to be found here. The river was vaulted over, and later the area became the cattle market (Veemarkt). The pretty wrought iron fences, designed by town architect Coomans according to a medieval pattern, were used for tying up cattle. Opposite this square, where the Hotel Ariane can now be found, there stood for many decades the slaughterhouse.

The reconstruction of this slaughterhouse in 1923, under Coomans' leadership, was no easy matter; the works first had to be postponed because there still stood 'Nissen huts' (semi-circular huts in corrugated iron) on the site. When they were eventually moved there was a railway strike preventing the construction materials from reaching the site. On the Veemarkt there is now just one reference to the busy construction activities during the years of the reconstruction. At number 7 there can be seen the warehouse of construction materials supplier Monkerhey-Van Neste dating from c.1928.

10 Minneplein 16: 'Villa Hélène'

This short street section that connects Veemarkt with Minneplein and already bears the latter's name, did not exist before the First World War. It is one of the few adjustments to the building plan that were made during the reconstruction. The corner house, Minneplein 16, is one of the few houses in Ypres built in the so-called 'cottage style'. A facing brick informs us that the house is called 'Villa Hélène'. In the garden façade, a beautiful art deco stained-

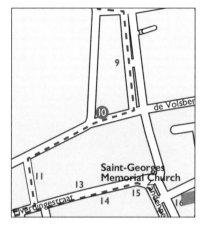

Minneplein, before 1914. (IWM)

MINNEPLEIN

After the demolition of the North-Western part of the ramparts during the Dutch Administration (1814–1830), Minneplein was created. The name 'Plaine d'Amour' for the new esplanade is supposed to have been a popular corruption of the name 'Plaine d'Armes'. Until the First World War, it was a large grassed square with picturesque characteristics. After the Armistice, the British briefly toyed with the idea of building a large international military cemetery here, but the grassed square was soon filled with emergency dwellings from the King Albert Fund. Along the centre's streets and squares, the temporary dwellings threatened to be in the way of the future reconstruction works. For several years, the real Ypres was to be found here: among the hundreds of huts one could find the Town Hall, St Martin's church, the state police barracks, and two schools. Now the square is occupied by a football field, sport halls and a number of schools.

glass window can be observed. The residence, which reminds us of the coastal architecture of the time, was built in 1927 according to a design by the architect, Depoorter. He was a Brussels man who came to Ypres during the reconstruction by governmental assignment. Depoorter was one of the few non-native architects not to leave after the reconstruction, but to stay in Ypres permanently.

Minneplein, 1919. (IWM)

11 Vestingstraat

One of the curious aspects of the reconstruction was that no use was made of the forced new start caused by the First World War to create a modern street plan. One might have expected that the new Ypres would get a grid pattern of wide boulevards, with an attempt to avoid narrow streets and illogical corners. But apart from a couple of examples that are not considered here in any depth, the medieval street plan of Ypres was reconstructed. This is the reason why the town centre still has narrow streets, such as this Vestingstraat. In the Middle Ages, this little street was called the 'Steendamstraetkin' after the little Steendam gate, knocked down

sometime around 1500. On the side of the Elverdingestraat we see on the short arch a little round arch niche which usually contains a statue of Our Lady with Child. The capstone mentions the date 5 September 1944, this was the day before the liberation of Ypres by Polish armoured troops during the Second World War.

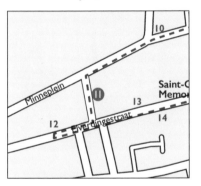

Above:
KAF huts on Minneplein.

Left: Minneplein, Vestingstraat and Elverdingestraat on the city map of Engel van Eeckhout, 1847.

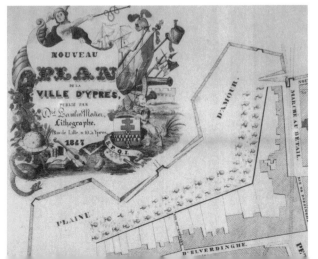

12 Elverdingestraat 50

This house is the Brussels architect Pierre Verbruggen's own residence. Like so many others, he was attracted by the high level of construction activity during the reconstruction and in 1923 he built this impressive residence in Ypres. The façade is plastered in cement on a base of pink natural stone. The façade surface is set off vertically by the stained glass windows mounted above each other. Above the door, there is a three-sided bay window. The terracotta semi-reliefs by Dolf Ledel portray a woman with sunflowers in front and two cherubs.

PIERRE VERBRUGGEN (1886–1940)

Before the First World War, the career of the modernistic Brussels architect Verbruggen had rapidly gone from strength to strength. But during the war years, the construction sector was all but inactive and Verbruggen kept himself busy with the organisation of conferences and simplified architectural courses aimed at a working class public. Like so many of his colleagues, he was tempted to the Devastated Regions by the busy building activities during the reconstruction. In contrast to many other master builders, he kept strictly to his own modernistic style that had little in common with the neo-Gothic propagated by the Ypres town architect Jules Coomans. Now and again, he made a concession to the more classic taste of his customers. This was for example the case with the 'Grand Bazar', Boterstraat 14, built in an eclectic style. Verbruggen is famous for his good knowledge of modern construction materials such as concrete. For a number of years, he was President of the Belgian Association for Modernistic Urbanists and Architects. Outside Ypres, he is mainly known for the Nautical College in Ostend (1931) and a number of villas in the Brussels capital region.

13 Elverdingestraat 32

The Georges Tack mansion, Elverdingestraat 32, is built in a neoclassical style. The mansard roof is interrupted by a pediment with a tablet and has two bulls'-eye windows. The house was built in typical yellow brick on a sandstone plinth. Since the end of the First World War, the plot on the east side of this house had remained undeveloped. It was only at the beginning of the 21st century that a house was built that, despite its contemporary appearance, is in harmony with its surroundings.

For the interior decoration of the Tack mansion, architect Frans Van Hove supplied a large number of designs, an activity that had been entrusted to him already before the First World War.

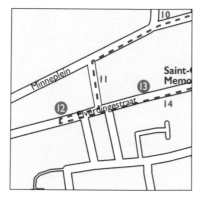

THE TACK FAMILY

After the Great War, the formerly well-known family Tack returned to their hometown, in contrast to most members of the local Ypres aristocracy and 'haute bourgeoisie'. Aside from the reconstruction of their houses, this extremely Catholic family handsomely financed the decoration of churches and chapels, from stained-glass windows, obits, and objects used in worship, to the restoration of memorial stones. Head of the family Georges Tack was for many years the president of the parish council of St Martin's church.

Elverdingestraat before the Great War. The picture was taken from the Tack mansion looking towards Herejanstraat. On the left side of the photo the buildings that would be replaced after the war by Elverdingestraat 13 and 15.

14 Elverdingestraat 13, 15 and 18

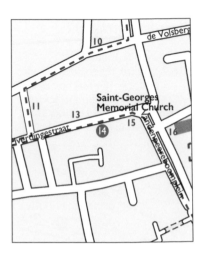

Nos 13 and 15 are both by the hand of architect Raphaël Speybrouck and date from 1924. Both residences show similarities in composition (five bays, a gate on the left, and a mansard roof punctuated by three windows). However, the finishing is completely different. Number 15 is very traditional and rigid; by contrast, number 13 has been given a modernistic accent and displays a certain playfulness. Indeed the house at number 13 was designed by the architect as his personal residence. On the opposite side, we see St Michael's School (Elverdingestraat 18). This little school complex first saw the light of day in 1922 to a design by architect M. Selly, but was only put into service as a school in 1930. Until that time, the temporary St Martin's Church was located here. Incidentally, the school buildings were built using old stones recuperated from the ruins of the old Church.

RAPHAËL SPEYBROUCK

Raphaël Speybrouck (born in Kortrijk on 14 April 1893) studied at the Saint Luke's Institute in Ghent, where he was awarded the first prize in 1919. He commenced his career at the Commissariat for the Reconstruction and so found his way to Ypres.

He mainly designed private houses. Between 1920 and 1928 he put his signature to 169 building plans, including Reigersburg Chateau in Brielen, Voddekasteel in Hollebeke and the tavern De Kolleblomme on the Market Square in Ypres. With respect for the image of the 'new' town that the then administration envisaged, his designs bear witness to historical accuracy. He only allowed himself more creative freedom when it came to his own home. In 1928 Van Speybrouck moved to the Belgian coast. He died near Antwerp on 26 June 1958.

The young architect Raphaël Speybrouck with his wife and daughter in front of their temporary dwelling in Ypres, 1921.

April 19, 1921: St Michael's school has already been rebuilt, the houses of Speybrouck opposite not yet.

15 Elverdingestraat 1–3: the former British Memorial School and St George's Memorial Church

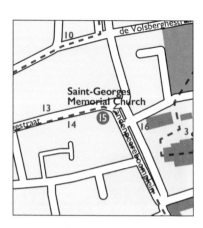

On the corner of the Elverdingestraat and the A. Vandenpeereboomplein, there is a little corner of Britain in Belgium. A herringbone brick path edged with wrought-iron fences takes us to the playground of the former British Memorial School. This little British school was built in 1927–1928 for the needs of the children of the British community in Ypres. In 1938 it had 99 pupils. The school was built as a memorial to the 342 Old Boys of Eton College who died in the war. Since the Second World War and up until the present day the school building has been in use as the meeting place for the British community in Ypres, which used to be predominantly composed of employees of the Commonwealth War Graves Commission (the organisation that looks after the maintenance of the British graves).

AN ANGLICAN CHURCH IN YPRES

It was Field Marshall French, 'Earl of Ypres', who, on 4 August 1924, the tenth anniversary of the outbreak of the Great War, launched the call for the building of an Anglican memorial church in Ypres. The Ypres League, a British association composed mainly of war veterans, organised the collection of donations and searched for a suitable site. The job of architect was given to Reginald Blomfield, who was already engaged with the design of the Menin Gate. After it became apparent that it would not be possible to realise initial spectacular plans for a church on top of the Lille Gate and the ramparts, negotiations were entered into with the widow of local nobleman Arthur Merghelynck regarding a plot of land on the corner of the A. Vandenpeereboomplein and the Elverdingestraat. Formerly, the private residence of Arthur Merghelynck, the founder of the museum of the same name, was located here. The purchase was concluded in September 1926, and on 24 July 1927, one hour after the inauguration of the Menin Gate, the first stone was laid.

Field Marshal Plumer places the first stone of St George's Memorial Church, 24 July 1927. (from the *Ypres Times*)

The Anglican St George's Memorial Church also thanks its existence mainly to the needs of the British community. The first stone was laid on the day the Menin Gate was unveiled (24 June 1927) and in 1929 the church was put into service. This single nave church with saddle roof is dominated on the exterior by the square tower in which the

Right: Arthur Merghelynck's mansion on the corner of A. Vandenpeereboomplein and Elverdingestraat would never be rebuilt but would make way for St George's Memorial Church.

Below: Australian troops passing in front of where after the war St George's Memorial Church will rise, 1918. (Australian War Memorial)

portal is also located. On the Vandenpeereboomplein, the semicircular fronton is crowned with a cross heavily reminiscent of the Cross of Sacrifice of the British military cemeteries. The reason this church is called a 'memorial church' can clearly be ascertained from the opulent interior: fabrics and furniture consist of objects of memorial to the British casualties of the First World War.

Left: St George's Memorial Church, c.1930.

Below: Sir Reginald Blomfield, architect of the Menin Gate and St George's Memorial Church on a photo taken on 24 July 1927.

SIR REGINALD BLOMFIELD

Both the school and the church were designed by Sir Reginald Blomfield, the architect of the Menin Gate. Blomfield (1856–1942), knighted in 1919, is one of the most important British architects of the 20th century. In London, Lambeth Bridge and the Piccadilly Circus Quadrant, among others, are his work; and in Oxford, the Lady Margaret Hall. After the First World War, Blomfield was one of the principal architects of the Imperial (later Commonwealth) War Graves Commission. In this capacity, he designed the Cross of Sacrifice, the Menin Gate, and countless individual cemeteries. His style displays a mix of classical and modern influences. Typical is the use of brick in a contracting combination with natural stone.

16 A. Vandenpeereboomplein 57: Kloosterpoort and Town Theatre

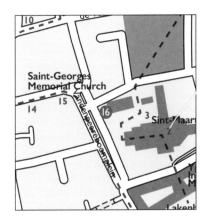

KLOOSTERPOORT (MONASTERY GATE)

Around 1780 J.B. Goossens, an architect from Ghent, who had been nominated shortly before as a teacher at the brand-new Ypres academy of fine arts, designed this new point of access to the St Martin's Monastery. The imposing entrance – which could formerly be closed off by means of massive wooden doors – was flanked on both sides by two Ionic pillars, on a sandstone base, supporting a triangular fronton. Between the fronton and the pillars there is a frieze with the inscription 'Claustrum Sti Martini' and in the fronton we see the coat of arms of the St Martin's Monastery. The ensemble is crowned by four stone urns. The monastery gate survived the First World War remarkably well and was restored in 1938.

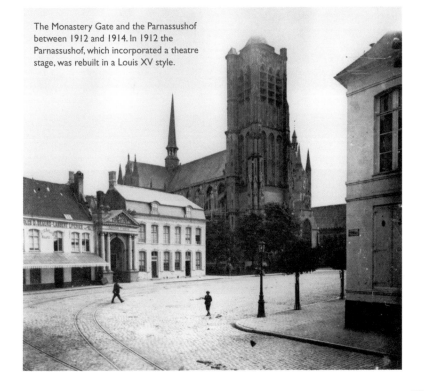

The Monastery Gate and the Parnassushof between 1912 and 1914. In 1912 the Parnassushof, which incorporated a theatre stage, was rebuilt in a Louis XV style.

THE TOWN THEATRE

On the southern side of Kloosterpoort is the town theatre. Before 1914, the Parnassushof was located here, a recreation facility which contained a theatre stage among other items. In 1912, the town converted the two recently acquired buildings between Kloosterpoort and St Martin's Church into one single building in the Louis XV style. After the war, a completely new theatre was built in 1931 after a design by Jules Coomans. The town architect did not in this case base himself on an existing pre-war building, but drew a new design in an eclectic architectural style dominated by neo-Gothic and neo-renaissance elements. Sculptures depicting the dramatic arts and music crown the various components of the front façade.

Above: The Monastery Gate in the last year of the war. (Australian War Memorial)

Below: The Monastery Gate in 1920.

A CONTROVERSIAL BUILDING

During the years of the reconstruction, the theatre was a source of friction between the ministerial Service for the Devastated Regions and the town administration. The town wished to see the pre-war Parnassushof rebuilt as early as 1926. However, economies prevented the Service for the Desvastated Regions from responding to the request.

In 1930, the 'Federation of the Afflicted' made the case flare up again when it demanded a large new theatre for Ypres. And some time later, when the building was almost finished, Inspector Smet of the Service for the Devastated Regions delivered a crushing verdict of Coomans' building: the acoustics were bad, the public could hardly see the stage, and he also had his doubts about the quality of the architecture. The inspector concluded: 'The building in no way fulfils its intention and has only been constructed with the aim of achieving an outward and for that matter very relative appearance, at the cost of its practical interior fittings'. But the theatre was anyway finished according to Coomans' plans.

17 Jules Coomansstraat: Monument in Memory of the Ypres War Casualties

This short street between A. Vanden-peereboomplein and Neermarkt has successively been called Aalstraat (until 1898) and Hallestraat. In 1938 it was given its current name in memory of the leading figure of the Ypres reconstruction who had died a year earlier. Before the First World War, the view of the medieval Meat Hall was limited by six small buildings. After the war, these houses were not rebuilt and the land that became free was used for the monument to the Ypres war casualties. The hundreds of civilians killed in Ypres during the war are not commemorated.

Before the war, six narrow houses stood on the site of the current Ypres War Memorial.

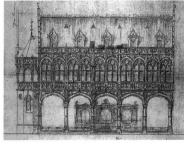

Above and right: Non-executed designs by Jules Coomans for a neo-Gothic echo of the 'Nieuwerck' with loggia surmounting the Ypres war memorial. The building was offered as an office to the War Graves Commission.

Left: The local newspaper *Het Ypersche/La Région d'Ypres* reports on the unveiling of the Ypres War Memorial, 3 July 1926.

In the 1920s, the 'Flemish Veterans' Association' (FVA) was a powerful Flemish Nationalist pressure group. On the day of the unveiling of the memorial, the FVA had been allocated a position at the back of the ceremonial procession and, much to their displeasure, there was no Flemish flag flying from the Town Hall. In the Boterstraat, where the FVA had taken their place, riots broke out. The mounted state police carried out a charge and several people were injured. Later too, when the FVA placed a floral tribute on the monument, the mounted state police attacked, breaking up the crowds with truncheons and brandished sabres. Here too, several people were injured and a number of FVA members were arrested. The Flemish press later emphasised the brutality of the state police and coined the phrase 'The Ypres Fury'. The name has survived and is still used by elder inhabitants of Ypres when they are talking about the war monument.

THE YPRES FURY

The unveiling of the Monument for the Ypres war casualties on Sunday 27 June 1926 was accompanied by vehement incidents, referred to as 'The Ypres Fury'. What happened?

The Ypres Fury: mounted gendarmerie stops the Flemish Veterans' Association from approaching the Ypres War Memorial, 27 June 1926.

The memorial was designed by town architect Jules Coomans in 1924 and executed by sculptor Alois De Beule (Ghent) between 1924 and 1926. The three-part wall monument in Belgian bluestone is given rhythm by pilasters with bronze figures of standing soldiers. In the middle we see the half-raised portrayal of a fallen soldier among women with laurel wreaths and a lying lion. On the left and right we see the bronze nameplates. The monument is topped off with decorative urns and the coat of arms of Ypres in the centre. The little flowerbed in front is cordoned off with a low wrought-iron fence. After the Second World War, nameplates were added lower down on the left and right.

The intention was for the war memorial to be located under an arcade over which a neo-Gothic variant of the Nieuwerck (Grote Markt) would be built. This 'loggia' would then also contain other memorial plaques and sculptures in remembrance of the war. Finally however, only one memorial plaque was installed, to the left of the monument: the plaque for the 7th and 13th Belgian Field Artillery, a Belgian unit attached to the British Army. Because a lack of funds prevented the construction of the building above the arcade, the town offered the plans in 1926 to the Imperial War Graves Commission so that it might build its offices there. The War Graves Commission turned the offer down, because 'it is improbable that we shall ever have a permanent office in Ypres'. Jules Coomans did not abandon his plans, and 10 years later, in 1936, he again proposed the construction of the building in order to house a museum. It was probably the death of the architect in 1937 that stopped the plans coming to fruition.

18 Neermarkt 8: The Meat Hall

It is believed that the lower floor of the 'Great Meat Hall' in natural stone was built in the second half of the 13th century. It refers clearly to the building characteristics of Cloth Hall and other similar medieval stone houses. The upper floor in brick dates only from

THE MULTIFARIOUS USES OF THE MEAT HALL

Although the cellars were rented to private individuals, the ground floor retained its original function right up to the Great War: the sale of meat. The first floor was used for a variety of purposes. For example, it was rented to the St Michael's guild of fencers, and between 1858 and 1914 it housed the Municipal Museum.

In December 1923, the town wanted to put the ground floor back into service as a meat hall, and the police station would be housed on the first floor. Eventually, the building was used as the Municipal Museum until 1974, after which it became a youth centre, and a complex of meeting and conference rooms. The first Ypres War Museum was built in the basement around 1930: a private initiative of the British war veteran Leo Murphy. At the outbreak of the Second World War the entire collection was shipped to Great Britain never to return.

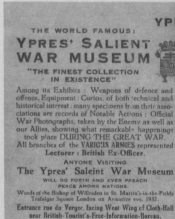

Publicity card for Leo Murphy's Ypres Salient War Museum, 1935.

1529. In the early months of the First World War, the building was razed to the ground. During those years, Coomans played with the idea of reconstructing the Meat Hall on a square with 'typical' Ypres façades. The loggia that he would later provide for the war monument then had to find a place on the side façade of the Meat Hall. Finally there followed in 1923 an extremely precise reconstruction, in which even the same types of wood were used, although it must be mentioned that the 'new' Meat Hall is 14 square metres smaller than the pre-war building, due to the new building line on Neermarkt.

Left and opposite: The Meat Hall, before and after the First World War.

No part of the Meat Hall was still standing at the end of the war. On the left we see the corner of the Cloth Hall, on the right the Yperlee river is flowing again in open air for the time being.

19 Boterstraat 14: The 'Grand Bazar'

The 'Bazar de la Rue au Beurre' or 'Grand Bazar' is a large shop with a distinctive urban character. The eye is immediately caught by the contiguous bay windows on the upper floors and the neo-baroque gable with its Art Deco flower decorations.

Its purpose as a trading house can clearly be seen in the large shop windows provided by the architect, Pierre Verbruggen. Verbruggen, most famous for his modernistic buildings, clearly played an eclectic card with this building. The construction work lasted from 1920 to 1923.

Boterstraat with the 'Grand Bazar' on the left, before 1914.

A DIFFICULT RECONSTRUCTION

The problems faced during the rebuilding of the 'Grand Bazar' are typical of many building programmes in the first few years of the reconstruction. Like so many of his peers, owner Jules Versailles in 1920 opts for a reconstruction by the Belgian state, i.e. by the Service for the Devastated Regions. He declares his agreement with the designs of architect Pierre Verbruggen and after navigating his way successfully through the red tape, the building is commissioned in June 1921. The design makes much use of reinforced concrete, so it is expected to proceed rapidly. But the winter of 1921–1922 is very harsh, and construction work is paused. To make matters worse, a heavy storm blows down the newly built walls. It isn't until April 1922 that the works can be resumed. In August 1922, the owner is at last able to move into a portion of the house. But then all sorts of technical problems surface. The marble fireplaces provided for in the plans turn out to be too expensive, and are substituted with granite ones. But the granite items take an age to arrive. Another reason that the building is delayed is the introduction of the 8–hour working day law. But following wide protests, the introduction of the law is postponed for construction work in the Devastated Regions. The 'Grand Bazar' is finally completed on 15 March 1923.

Left: The reconstruction of Boterstraat in full swing. On the right the already finished facade of the new 'Grand Bazar', c.1922–23.

20 # Between Boterstraat 21,23: Vispoort

The original Vispoort (Fish Gate) or Neptune's Gate was in Louis XIV style and dated from 1714, the last year of a long period of Ypres under French rule. The relief work was by the renowned Ypres sculptor Louis Ramaut. Although the reconstruction plans of Jules Coomans are dated 1923, the work is

A CONTROVERSIAL SCULPTURE

In the 1920s and 1930s, the Vispoort looks rather bare without a sculpture. In 1937, the town administration comes to the decision that enough time has passed and requests the reconstruction of the relief. Henry Van de Velde – artistic advisor to the Minister of Public Works – is asked for his opinion regarding the aptness of these works. The world-famous architect answers, 'The design lacks any artistic value.' In his opinion, every creative artist will refuse such a commission, and he proposes replacing the relief work with a simple inscription and coat of arms topped with an architectural pinnacle. But the town administration does not waver. The work is eventually done by the Ypres sculptor Maurice Deraedt. It is no easy task. Due to the fact that a neighbouring building has received an additional storey, the surface to be sculpted above the entrance has changed. Deraedt therefore

Above: The Vispoort before 1914.

Opposite: Jules Coomans' design for the reconstruction of the Vispoort.

has to operate more vertically than horizontally. His relief shows a number of differences from the original: the sea god no longer looks at passers-by but straight ahead. Today's relief also has far fewer details than the original. There are a couple of anecdotes regarding the creation of the relief. For example, Deraedt is supposed to have searched high and low for a suitable person to model the rough appearance of the raging Neptune. Finally, he found the ideal model in the person of local lifeguard Van Uxem. The slaughterhouse vet provided a muscular racing horse as a model for the horse pulling the wagon. But the animal was jumpy, so to calm it down, it was given beer to drink.

MDCCXIV

postponed due to its non-urgent nature. The gate is constructed temporarily in concrete blocks, and only gained its current appearance at the end of the

1920s. The half-raised sculpturing is only added ten years later, in 1938. Just as in pre-war times, the sculpture depicts an episode from Vergil's Aeneid: during a ferocious storm whipped up by wind gods, the fleet of Aeneas is split up, and Neptune, god of the sea, rises out of the water, seated in a wagon pulled by horses of the sea, and calms the storm. The arched cornice is topped by the town's coat of arms between a pair of fish. The ceiling of the passage to the Vismarkt is finished in concrete, in contrast to the 18th century appearance of the gate.

Left: Boterstraat, 29 June 1923. The Vispoort is already there, albeit finished with breeze blocks.

Below: Sculptor Maurice Deraedt poses in front of his shop and studio in A. Merghelynckstraat.

MAURICE DERAEDT

Sculptor Maurice Deraedt is born on 30 April 1881 in Ypres, the son of a baker in Elverdingestraat. He studied at the academies of Ypres, Lille, and Antwerp. Following the death of his father he is obliged to give up his studies and take over the bakery in order to provide for his extended family (11 brothers and sisters), but he never stopped sculpting. Even when working in a French munitions factory during the war, he still found time to make wooden sculptures. After the war, Deraedt stayed in France, working as a frame-maker. Attracted by the busy reconstruction activities in Ypres, he returned in 1924, with the ambition of making it as a sculptor. It is to be no easy task because town architect Jules Coomans prefers to give commissions to his former fellow students from the St Luke's School in Ghent like Alois De Beule and Oscar Sinia. But Deraedt finds work

with Edouard Froidure (see number 4), who entrusts him with all the sculpture work for his houses and chapel. This affords Deraedt a little fame, and from the end of the 1920s, he is involved in the reconstruction of other houses and monuments. For example, the sculpture work for the Belle Alms House complex (see number 23) is entrusted to him, and along with the Vispoort it would be the pinnacle of his career. Throughout his life he always remains a simple, traditional sculptor of ornaments and, now and again, a statue. In 1955, Maurice Deraedt dies of a chronic illness.

21 Vismarkt and Minckhuisje

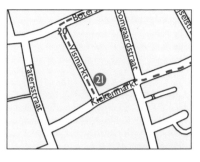

From the Vispoort/Neptune's Gate you reach Vismarkt (Fish Market), laid out following the vaulting over of the Yperlee in 1714. The elegant wrought iron pre-war sales stalls were replaced in 1923 with frankly rather cumbersome bluestone constructions topped with hipped roofs, designed – again – by Jules Coomans. The latter was also responsible for one of the most curious buildings in Ypres, an anachronistic folly, the so-called 'Minckhuisje'. Designed by the town architect in 1899 as a toll booth in a very decorative neo-Gothic style, it was rebuilt in 1923. The building has been unoccupied for many decades.

Above: Vismarkt and Minckhuisje before 1914.

22 Rijselstraat 27

The shop premises at Rijselstraat 27 have a cemented cornice with neo-classicist leanings. At the level of the first floor in the building, the pilasters are decorated with allegorical portrayals of mythical animals and busts of people's heads. Further up, Silvère Reynaert, owner and resident of the building, had his name inscribed in the façade. Here, he operated a stove shop. The top floor has a bay window.

The house is a typical example of the multiple application, during the reconstruction, of all sorts of often unexpected inscriptions and decorations on the façade.

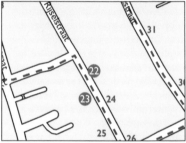

'ZUUDSTRAETE' (SOUTH STREET)
In 1992, a very original initiative took place in the Rijselstraat. Shopkeepers and residents had the old – and usually forgotten – house names reinstated. For example, the house at number 27 was formerly called 'Leopoldus'. Rijselstraat, which was called 'Zuudstraete' or South Street in the Middle Ages, has always been one of the main arteries

Rijselstraat, looking from the corner with Burchtstraat in the direction of the Cloth Hall, 29 June 1923.

through the town. It linked the two important town centres of Grote Markt and St Peter's Church, and then led on via the now vanished suburb of St Michael outside the Lille Gate to Lille.

23 | Rijselstraat 38: Belle Alms House

The former Belle Alms House, Rijselstraat 38, was for decades – and until March 2016 – the administrative office of the Ypres Public Centre for Social Welfare, while the chapel was fitted out as a museum. Now this is still an exhibition space. The Belle Alms House was built around 1273 by Christine de Guines, the widow of Salomon Belle, as a foundation for the relief of the poor during a crisis period in the Ypres textile industry. In 1616, a new chapel was built. During the war, the complex was thoroughly destroyed, and a large number of works of art were

fortunately saved in the nick of time. After the war, the chapel was carefully reconstructed from 1923 on, according to the plans of Jules Coomans. The chapel is a typical example of late-Gothic architecture with renaissance ornaments. On the left and right respectively, we see the coats of arms of the Belle and de Guines families. On the left, there is also a bronze plaque by Maurice Deraedt in honour of surgeon Jan Yperman, who worked here around 1300, and is the author of the oldest Dutch tract on medicine. On the left and right of the large window, the kneeling figures of founders Salomon Belle and Christine de Guines are portrayed. These works were carried out

Left: Belle Alms House before the war.

Above: Belle Alms House during the war.

Belle Alms House, 1919. (IWM)

by Alois De Beule, based on pre-war models. Jef Dekeyser's reconstruction of the statue of St Nicholas on the middle pillar only took place at the beginning of the 21st century!

The four shops to the right of the chapel look a bit anachronistic with their uniform wooden doors, small shop fronts, and wrought iron signboards. The buildings belong to the Social Welfare Centre, which explains their uniform appearance. In his designs of 1924, architect G. Lernould largely restored the pre-war appearance.

THE 'ONGOING' RECONSTRUCTION

The statue of St Nicholas that adorned the façade of the Belle Alms House before the First World War was only rebuilt at the beginning of the 21st century. It was by no means the only piece of Ypres' history that re-joined the urban heritage many decades after the war. For example, until recently some plots of land in the city centre remained undeveloped. Many of the original owners never returned from exile and – due to the destruction of the archives – the rightful owners were not known. These gaps in the urban fabric were only filled between 2001 and 2019!

And with a bit of goodwill, the phenomenon of war souvenirs making the journey back home decades later can also be seen as a contribution to the ongoing reconstruction of the city. Hardly a month passes without the Ypres museums or St Martin's Church being rejoiced by a foreign donor – those with an object that their ancestor had found as a soldier in the ruins and taken home as a souvenir, but which the descendants now believe belongs in this city.

A medieval console and a piece of stained glass, taken as a war souvenir and returned to the city of Ypres many decades later. From the collection of In Flanders Fields Museum.

24 Rijselstraat 33

This imposing building in the Louis XV style was constructed in 1925 according to a design probably by Jules Coomans. Here, what we are looking at is the reconstruction of a house that was located in the Sint-Jacobsstraat prior to the First World War, namely the 'de Lichtervelde mansion', which was occupied in 1914 by burgomaster René Colaert.

Originally, this building was the local pub of the Catholic Circle, and was called the 'Patria'. Note that there is natural stone incorporated into this façade, including above all the doors, windows, and in the pediment. In 1925, the Ypres sculptor Maurice Deraedt was awarded the job of carrying out the decorations: he first delivered the two lovely wooden doors and drew the designs in the rocaille style for all the coping stones. But due to lack of funds, the works were never completed. That is why the heavy blocks of natural stone still await a sculptor's skills …

Left: The pre-war facade of the 'de Lichtervelde' mansion in Sint-Jacobsstraat which heavily inspired the reconstruction at Rijselstraat 33.

25 Rijselstraat 56–58: The Former Lamotte School

This quite faithful reconstruction (a listed monument) of a double residence is based on an original built in 1606. In 1695, the nuns of Onze-Lieve-Vrouw-ten-Bunderen occupied these buildings, which was refitted as a girls' school in 1785: the Free Girls' School Foundation of Zuutpeene Lamotte (still referred to today as the 'Lamotjes'). In 1873, the nuns were

Yper, fondatie Lamothe — Fondation Lamothe, Ypres.

Above: The reconstruction of the former Lamotteschool in its final phase, 29 June 1923.

Left: The former Lamotte School before the First World War, with a picture of the foundress of the foundation.

expelled at the command of the liberal town administration, and the town girls' school was established here. The houses, flattened in the First World War, were reconstructed in 1923, by Jules Coomans again. Both houses were strikingly built in red brick, with yellow brick used for pretty decorative motifs. After the reconstruction and up to the 1950s, the buildings served as the residence of the headmistress of the town girls' school. They are both in private ownership now.

26 The intersection of Rijselstraat – Sint-Elisabethstraat – A. Merghelynckstraat

The Merghelynck Museum, an 18th century building forming the southern corner between the Rijselstraat and the A. Merghelynckstraat, has determined the post-war appearance

of this intersection. Despite the fact that the museum itself was only rebuilt from 1932, the architects of the three other corners took the neo-classicist appearance of the pre-war museum building into account in their designs, along with the building materials used (yellow brick combined with natural stone). This has led to the creation of a pretty, balanced, and yet architecturally diverse intersection.

The large house on the other side of the Rijselstraat (number 62) has been attractively rebuilt with recycled materials. Designed by the Brussels architect M. Selly, it was in the early 1920s the property of Royal High Commissioner De Schoonen who co-ordinated the Reconstruction of Ypres.

Café Het Zilveren Hoofd.

HET ZILVEREN HOOFD (THE SILVER HEAD)

This 'reconstruction by imitation' style is most clearly seen in the tavern 'Het Zilveren Hoofd' (Rijselstraat 49), designed in 1922 by A. Taurel, a Walloon architect who based himself in Ypres in the 1920s, along with so many others. Just like the museum opposite, the tavern is constructed from yellow bricks on a plinth of sandstone from Arras. The façades are given rhythm by colossal pilasters. A striking element is that a medallion was placed over the door during the reconstruction, showing the silver-plated head of King Albert I of Belgium. But the name of the tavern pre-dates this considerably, and it is the medallion that refers to the name, not the other way round. This use of the image of the King as an ornament was not unique during the reconstruction. A house in the G. De Stuersstraat has a

bust of Albert I at the top of its façade and the King is also portrayed over the Donkerpoort at the Cloth Hall.

Above: The reconstruction of Rijselstraat 62 is nearing completion, 20 July 1921.

Below: Design for café Het Zilveren Hoofd by architect A. Taurel, June 1922. (Collection Charles Vermeulen)

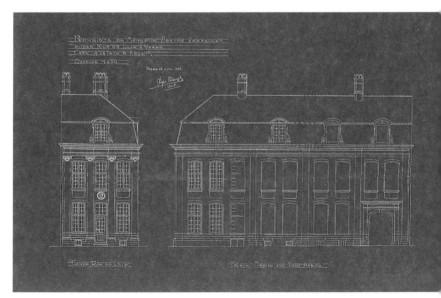

27 Rijselstraat 64

This private house on the corner with Sint-Elisabethstraat dates from 1930. After the war, this area remained undeveloped for quite a while, and there were huts and a church of the U.S. Army here. Eventually, the land was bought by Doctor W. Van den Bussche who had a house built to a plan by architect Minnens. As with the other corner buildings, yellow bricks were employed, this time on a plinth in bluestone. The unbroken shopfront and cornices on the upper floors determine the horizontal façade division. The rounded bay window is topped with a decorative bulls-eye, surrounded by rocaille motifs. The woodwork of the door is very accomplished. All the decorative sculpture of this imposing neo-rococo façade is the work of Maurice Deraedt. In particular the keystone of the door opening is

remarkable: it shows the face of the former owner Doctor W. Van den Bussche. Also striking is the contrast between this neo-rococo front façade and the more modernistic side façade in Sint-Elisabethstraat.

Above: The face of Doctor W. Van den Bussche above the door of his house, Rijselstraat 64.

28 Rijselstraat 70

The former post office building is also sometimes called the High House or the Templars' Hall. The last name is a misnomer, because there has never been a house of the Templars at this location. The post office was constructed from 1897 to 1903 out of two buildings bought by the state. The

The 13th-century stone house in Rijselstraat by Auguste Böhm, c.1847.

THE FORMER POST OFFICE BUILDING

At the end of 1918, the post office was one of the very few buildings in town still – for the most part – standing. But there is great difficulty in maintaining a ruin. In March 1920, it was realised that much of the stone and building material had been removed from the post office building for re-use elsewhere. Upon this realisation, complete reconstruction was undertaken without anymore delays. The management of the post office first wanted an artist to commit his artistic impressions of the majestic ruins to canvas. The idea was for this painting to be hung in the main hall of the reconstructed post office building. These plans, however, came to nought. In the autumn of 1920, work commenced under the direction of the legendary Ypres contractor Alphonse Angillis, nicknamed 'bear Angillis' after his substantial build.

In the basement of the former post office there is a unique memento of life in the besieged Ypres of November 1914. In the wall there is a rectangular memorial plaque with the text: 'Albert Lemay. Born on this spot 24–11–1914'.

Albert Lemay next to the memorial plaque in the basement of the post office building.

The same building shortly after its restoration and transformation into a post office, c. 1900.

house on the left, and depicted on p65, was the so-called Templars' Hall, a medieval stone house dating from the 13th century. This building – the architectural style of which shows similarities with Cloth Hall and the Meat Hall – was drawn by the artist A. Böhm in the middle of the 19th century. During the construction of the post office building, the Templars' Hall was restored in a hard manner as was the custom at the time. The house on the right – that had a simple cornice – was incorporated in the reconstruction of the building.

During the First World War, the building was not completely destroyed thanks to the strength of the walls in Arras sandstone. The carpentry of the rafters was also spared. It was thus possible to restore the building completely as it was before the war. The works were undertaken in May 1920, and were completed at the start of 1923. On 4 February of that year, the new post office was inaugurated. It would remain functional here until the late 1990s.

The post office building in 1919.

29 Merghelynck Museum

The Merghelynck Hotel was built in 1774 to a design by the Lille architect Thomas Gombert at the behest of Frans Merghelynck, hereditary treasurer and high bailiff of the city of Ypres. At the end of the 19th century, it became a museum. In 1915 the building was completely flattened, and in 1932–1934 reconstruction work began under the leadership of the architects J.

The Merghelynck Museum before the First World War.

The few remains of the Merghelynck Museum after the First World War with the ruins of the post office building in the background.

Cloquet and P. Saintenoy. The museum is composed of a number of buildings grouped around a courtyard. The building material used for this listed monument is yellow brick on a plinth of Arras sandstone. Sandstone was also used for the sculpted elements. This delicate and balanced mansion is built in a transitional rococo/neo-classical style, in which the rococo influences are best seen in the decorations, for example on the pediment above the carriage entrance.

Exhibition of rescued objects from the Merghelynck Museum at the Petit Palais in Paris, 6 March 1916.

THE PERILOUS JOURNEY OF A MUSEUM'S COLLECTION DURING AND AFTER THE FIRST WORLD WAR

Arthur Merghelynck – great-grandson of the building's commissioner – opened a museum at this location in 1894, dedicated to the refined lifestyle of the aristocracy in the 18th century. On his death in 1908, the Royal Academy of Belgium became the museum's new owner. In 1915, the building was razed to the ground, but a large proportion of its contents was saved in the nick of time by the 'Dhuicque Mission' of the Belgian government. It's rich collection was first transferred to Le Havre, seat of the Belgian government in exile, and then to Le Touquet-Paris-Plage, the place of exile of the Ypres municipal administration. Finally, parts of the collection were exhibited for a few years in the Petit Palais in Paris. After the war, the collection was moved to the cellars of the provincial government building in Bruges, and then to the cellars of the Royal Museums for Art and History in the Parc Cinquantenaire in Brussels. But when the reconstruction of the museum was completed in 1934, there was no budget left. The refitting of the museum was put on indefinite hold. After being used as a school during the Second World War, things only got moving again in 1951. In the meantime, many of the museum's objects had been irreparably damaged in the frequent moves. The museum finally opened its doors in June 1956.

30 D'Hondtstraat 37

According to its unsigned building
permit request, this house dates from
1921–1922. This is also confirmed
by the striking inscriptions over
the windows of the first floor: '1914
oorlog' [war], '1915
slecht' [bad], '1918
vrede' [peace], '1922
recht' [upright]. Again
on a basis of these
inscriptions, we can
hypothesise that the
house that stood here
before the Great War
was destroyed in 1915 by
its ravages. Left and right
of the central stepped
gable, an extension of
questionable taste was
added.

THE D'HONDTSTRAAT

This old street (first mentioned in 1217
as 'Hontstrata') has always been a narrow,
cobbled street with a slight bend. Nothing
changed in the reconstruction, including a
number of extremely narrow alleys. Only in

the vicinity of Grote Markt was the street
straightened and widened. D'Hondtstraat is
one of the few streets in the town to have
multiple façades that survived the shells of
the First World War. Just as in pre-war times,
the street plays an important residential role.

D'Hondtstraat in 1919. Nowhere else in Ypres had
so many facades that more or less survived the war.

31 D'Hondtstraat 21: The 'Genthof'

The 'Genthof' is a building in late Gothic style with renaissance influences, dating from the second half of the 16th century. The double stepped gable in yellow brick is punctuated by pointed arch windows on the ground floor and round arch windows on the first floor. The execution of the gable tops with profiled steps and twisted pinnacles is typical of the Flemish Renaissance.

The 'Genthof' before the First World War.

THE 'DHUICQUE MISSION'

In the neutral Belgium of 1914, there existed no plans to bring works of art, church treasures, and archives to a place of safety in times of war. Nobody foresaw the devastating effect of modern artillery on the architectural heritage.

So at the start of the First World War, safeguarding and conservation of heritage was taken up by private individuals. On 20 May 1915, the architect Eugène Dhuicque, a specialist in medieval architecture, was appointed by the Belgian government as the head of a rescue operation in the small corner of Belgium still unoccupied by the enemy. His mission was to save what could be saved. Everything which couldn't be transported and was under threat of destruction had to be photographed and inventoried. Dhuicque created an enormous collection of photographs that bear witness to the destruction of Ypres and other places in the Westhoek region. He also built up a large collection of architectural drawings of buildings destroyed by the war. After the war, Eugène Dhuicque had a say in the debate of whether or not to rebuild Ypres. He advocated the conservation of the ruins of the Cloth Hall and St Martin's Church in a 'zone of silence'.

Belgian engineers of the 'Dhuicque Mission' consolidate the ruins of the Cloth Hall, 1917.

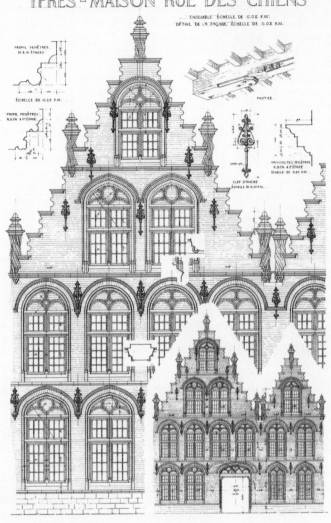

YPRES = MAISON RUE DES CHIENS

The 'Genthof', as recorded by the
'Dhuicque Mission' during the war.

Note also the heart-shaped wall
anchors. In 1904, it was restored.
All that effort was not completely in
vain, because after the First World
War, the façade of the Genthof –
although severely damaged – was not
completely destroyed. For reasons of

art history, the 'Dhuicque Mission' of
the Belgian government had extensively
photographed and sketched the
house during the war. It was restored
according to the pre-war plans.

In addition, the façade of the house
at number 23 (the former district
commissioner's office) survived the war,
although it was very badly damaged.
The building is a fine example of the
classicist appearance.

32 Grote Markt 31: 'Au Carillon'

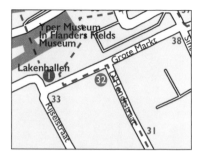

This eclectic corner house by D'Hondtstraat is the work of architect A. Maegerman from Boulogne-sur-Mer (France). It dates from 1922. The corner bay is bevelled off and contains the entrance door to the shop. The shop front consists of marble on a bluestone

The Cloth Hall on fire, 22 November 1914. (Antony d'Ypres)

plinth. The rest of the house is brick built and accentuated with Euville stone. The house has a mansard roof laid with slate. The gable is edged with scrollwork and topped with vase-shaped decorations. We are struck by the medallions in the display windows and above the shop doors with depictions of the pre-war Rijselstraat with St Peter's Church, the pre-war Cloth Hall, the fire of the Cloth Hall on 22 November 1914, and the Cloth Hall in ruins. These stained glass windows are signed by A. De Coninck from Kortrijk.

THE FIRE OF THE CLOTH HALL ON 22 NOVEMBER 1914

The fire of the Cloth Hall, which is depicted in a medallion on the 'Au Carillon' house, took place on 22 November 1914. It is often written that the German troops set the Cloth Hall and St Martin's Church ablaze with incendiary shells out of frustration at not being able to break through at Ypres. In any case, the fire of the Cloth Hall of Ypres was one of the most publicly abhorred 'deeds of German barbarity' in the history of the First World War, just as the fire of the Louvain university library had been a few months previously.

There was not a single newspaper in the Allied world that did not publish the famous picture of the Antony brothers. The population of Ypres also considered the fire of the Cloth Hall as the lowest and saddest point of the shelling of their town. Sister Marguerite-Marie (Emma Boncquet) of the Lamotte school wrote in her diary: 'Heavy fire at about 6 o'clock in the morning. By 9, the Hall was under fire. The first shell fell on the tower, the third on the clock. At about 11 o'clock the carillon collapsed and the Hall was ablaze. It is a horrible spectacle. In a moment the building is a great sea of flames. Then St Martin's Church also went up.' In the fire, the extensive medieval archive of the town was lost, along with many paintings.

33 Grote Markt 43–45: The 'Regina'

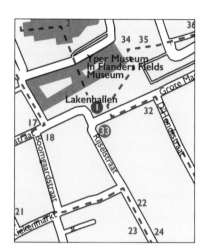

On the corner of Grote Markt and Rijselstraat stood for a long time the imposing wooden house 'de Wissele'. It was replaced in the course of the 19th century by a stone construction. After the war, the Scheerlinck brothers, who were working for Jules Coomans, designed this hotel and adjoining commercial building as one ensemble in replacement of three pre-war buildings. It was to turn out as a neo-Gothic construction with a recessed niche on the south-west corner in which the statue of an angel with sword (possibly St Michael) stands. This niche is a striking reference to the former wooden building, which had in the same place an imposing statue of the Madonna with Jesus on her left arm that dominated the streetscape. The commercial building at Grote Markt 43 is another Ypres building that mentions the dates of destruction and reconstruction above the shop front.

BATTLEFIELD TOURISM

The fact that the corner house at the intersection of Grote Markt and Rijselstraat was turned into a hotel during the years of the reconstruction should not come as a surprise. In the period immediately following the end of the war, not only did the previous inhabitants come and take a look, but the place was also swarming with tourists, not just those Belgians who had the means to make the trip, but also pilgrims from elsewhere – Britain in particular. From 1919 onwards, commercial minds had various guides and maps printed up showing the way to the ruins, the battlefields, and the cemeteries. Others organised day trips to the devastated region. The 'afflicted' did not resist, because they could also gain from the influx. Cafés and hotels (and war museums) shot up like mushrooms. At first this new hospitality and tourist industry was found in scattered huts, before moving

Above: The houses at the corner of Grote Markt and Rijselstraat before 1914.

Right: The Regina under construction, 24 March 1922.

A tourist snapshot of Grote Markt in 1919, at that time already a starting point for excursions to the former battlefields.

to new buildings in front of the Menin Gate, at the station, or – as here – on Grote Markt. Many foreigners seized the opportunity of making some money in the area. The many ceremonies, inaugurations of new buildings and monuments, visits by high officials, and organised British pilgrimages all led to people arriving in their droves. In contrast to the construction works, tourism continued to represent a sustainable source of income.

34 ## Grote Markt 32, 30, 28: 'Het Klein Stadhuis' – 'Den Anker' – 'In de Trompet'

The fine façades of the three taverns closest to the 'Nieuwerck' are faithful reconstructions of the pre-war situation. In the case of 'Het Klein Stadhuis' we can even speak of a double reconstruction, because the gable had to be rebuilt again after the Second World War. The year tablets of 1924 and 1952 bear witness to this. In the frontage of the café you can vaguely see a shadow of the short façade of 'Nieuwerck'. Unfortunately there remains no trace of the pre-war cellar space, half raised above street level. The

Left: 'Het Klein Stadhuis' and 'Den Anker' before before the First World War.

Below: Designs by Frans Van Hove for the facades of 'Het Klein Stadhuis', 'Den Anker' and 'In de Trompet', May 1919.

FRANS VAN HOVE

Frans Van Hove (Ghent 1872–1939) worked all his life in the shadow of Jules Coomans. He was already assisting the town architect before the war broke out. Van Hove was also a proponent of a traditional style during the reconstruction. He mainly designed residential and commercial buildings, including the taverns 'Het Klein Stadhuis' and 'Den Anker', and 'In den Trompet' on the Grote Markt. For the Tack House (number 13) he designed the interior.

Above: French officers during a parade on Grote Markt, December 1914. Unlike the 'Nieuwerck' on the left, the facades of 'Het Klein Stadhuis', 'Den Anker' and 'In de Trompet' have not yet suffered any damage.

façade of 'Den Anker' originally dates from 1611 and is an exponent of the local renaissance style. In 1922 it was reconstructed, although the pre-war brick decoration and profiled chimney were omitted. 'In de Trompet' was also a tavern in the local renaissance style and was reconstructed in 1922. The house has embellished wall anchors and in the gable we can see next to the aedicula window the depictions of sun and moon. The three taverns are the work of Jules Coomans' assistant Frans Van Hove, among others.

35 Grote Markt 22

This former residence – which since 1936 has been successively shop and restaurant – is dated 1927, as witnessed by the stone in the gable. The building has an eclectic stepped gable in yellow

THE CURIOUS ORNAMENTATION OF GROTE MARKT 22

This house was, like the house at Surmont de Volsberghestraat 13 (see number 4), another property belonging to Edouard 'hunchback' Froidure. The idea behind the façade-wide loggia was to provide a location for the future bishops of Ypres to bless the population. Froidure – whose son was a priest – never gave up the fervent hope that Ypres would one day again become the seat of a bishopric.

As a result of his great devotion for Mary, he placed an order with sculptor Deraedt for a relief portraying the Madonna with Child which was installed in the gable. The Latin text around the relief says: 'Queen Mother of Christ-King. Patroness of Hungary and Ypres'. The parapet thus shows on the left the coat of arms of Hungary and on the right that of Ypres. Above the Hungarian coat of arms, which is being held by two angels, there is a text in Hungarian.

In imitation of Greenwich, the eccentric amateur astronomer Froidure would talk about an 'Ypres meridian'. So the tablet on the middle parapet indicates the meridian of Ypres. The line formed by the shadow, which is cast by the iron arrow on the arched stone on the middle parapet at 12 o'clock midday precisely, indicates the meridian, explains the Latin text next to the arrow.

Opposite: An arrow on the parapet of Grote Markt 22 indicates the 'Ypres meridian'. On the left the coat of arms of the kingdom of Hungary, on the right that of the city of Ypres.

brick that incorporates simili and Euville stones. At the level of the second floor there is a loggia with an arcade on pillars and a parapet. Some elements refer to local Gothic and renaissance patterns – pointed arches, three-lobed embellishments, and diagonal top pieces. The many sculptures on the façade are again the work of the Ypres sculptor Maurice Deraedt.

Also worthy of note is the Café Central on the other side of the corner of the Diksmuidestraat. What is striking about this house by architect O. Depoorter is the Art Nouveau tinged decoration. The year tablet of 1929 betrays that this house was reconstructed quite late, probably pending the definitive building line.

Edouard Froidure, nicknamed 'hunchback' Froidure, the pious catholic owner of both this property and the mansion at Surmont de Volsberghestraat 13 (see no. 4).

36 Grote Markt 10: The 'Kasselrijgebouw' (Castellany Building)

The 'Kasselrij' building was constructed at this location in 1551. It was one of the prettiest and largest buildings on Grote Markt, with seven half-raised portrait busts on the first floor that represented the seven – then known – planets. In 1914, the building had a plastered façade and the roof was edged with a wrought-iron balustrade. The 'Kasselrij' building was reconstructed from 1921 onwards in a history-

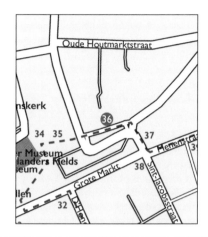

Until the completion of the reconstruction of the Cloth Hall in 1967, the rebuilt 'Kasselrij' building functioned as the town hall.

A RICH HISTORY

The 'Kasselrij' building was the sheriffs' house of the Ypres Castellany until the institution was abolished during the French Revolution. In 1810 the building was sold to the town. Until 1914, it was the location of the popular 'Hôtel de la Châtellenie', the home of many a lavish banquet. It also housed the literary association La Concorde, which had at its disposal a number of features including a fabulous reading room in Louis XV style. After the reconstruction, the 'Kasselrij' building was taken into use by the city as a provisional Town Hall until the 'Nieuwerck', part of the Cloth Hall, was completed in 1967. The building now houses the Corporate Court.

inspired manner to a design by Jules Coomans, who had already worked out a proposal for the building in 1916.

The building is now much more severe than it ever was before. Inspired by old documents, Coomans replaced the delicate wrought-iron balustrade by a cumbersome version in Euville stone and he strew three rows of dormer windows over the roof. The elegant portrait busts were replaced by medallions by the hand of Alois De Beule, and now portrayed the seven deadly sins. From left to right we recognise pride, greed, lust, envy, gluttony, wrath, and sloth.

Right: A postcard from 1914 with the 'Kasselrij' building in undamaged condition and the condition after the first shellings.

Left: 'Lust', one of the seven deadly sins that Aloïs De Beule sculpted for the reconstructed facade of the 'Kasselrij' building.

37 Grote Markt 1: Court of Justice

The eastern side of Grote Markt is now occupied by the Court of Justice. This is where the Hospital of Our Lady stood until 1914. The new Court of Justice was designed – again – by Jules Coomans, and was built between 1924 and 1930 as an eclectic construction in which local Gothic and renaissance style characteristics intertwine. Here too, the typical yellow brick was used.

The building is decorated with sculptures by Alois De Beule. In the middle there is a relief depicting the Judgement of Solomon with two large

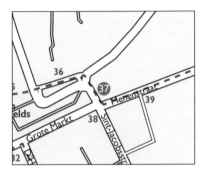

statues on the left and right – Justice and Wisdom. Above the entrance porch we see the Belgian coat of arms with the inscription 'Eendracht maakt macht' [Union is Strength].

The almost completed building of the Court of Justice, c. 1929.

A WIDE ARRAY OF INSTITUTIONS

The Court of First Instance had since 1841 been housed in the former Bishop's Palace, behind St Martin's Church. This beautiful residence in the French style was, however, not reconstructed. At the start of the 20th century, it was also no longer considered appropriate to have a hospital in the very centre of the town, for reasons of hygiene. Therefore, from 1922 the Our Lady's Hospital was moved to the northern edge of town – on Lange Torhoutstraat. In its place, a new courthouse was constructed.

Top: The pre-war Our Lady's Hospital. The small wall and the side gate on the left survived the war and still stands today.

Above: On the east side of Grote Markt, the remains of the Our Lady's Hospital dominate the otherwise empty square, 1919. (IWM)

38 The gable row on the side of Grote Markt

The houses of Grote Markt – in this case on the southern side – do not display many similarities with the pre-war façades. The old photographs show mainly classicist, late-classicist, and simple 19th century façades, including ensembles in unitary construction. Today Grote Markt is dominated by

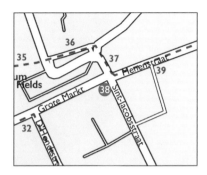

Fair on the rebuilt Grote Markt. Due to the corner of Coomans' Court of Justice not the entire Menenstraat is visible.

A VIEW TO THE MENIN GATE

From this corner of Grote Markt, a good view is to be had of the Menin Gate. Before the war this would not have been possible because the Menenstraat had a bend in it. It is possible that the bend was straightened out during the reconstruction in order to accommodate the requests of the British. After all, for a long time the British government wanted a memorial on Grote Markt, besides the Menin Gate, either in the form of preserved ruins or in the form of

an architectural monument. The Belgian side was not completely accommodating, though: Reginald Blomfield, architect of the Menin Gate, remembers in his memoirs that he asked his Ypres confrere Jules Coomans to make some adjustments to his Courthouse. This would allow a beautiful direct view from the centre of the Cloth Hall to the Menin Gate. Coomans refused and therefore a direct view between Ypres two most important monuments is impossible.

A view of the south side of Grote Markt from the belfry tower, 15 August 1909.

variants of traditional building patterns which are mainly based on Gothic and local renaissance style.

On the corner of Menenstraat and Sint-Jacobsstraat – on the opposite side from the Court of Justice – the 'Yperley' with its neo-rococo appearance is an exception to the rule. This former bank building was built as an 18th century 'hôtel' after the French pattern. The initials BN on the little corner turret stand for 'Banque Nationale', because the National Bank of Belgium had a branch here for some time.

The house at Grote Markt 3 has unusual wall anchors. They give the year of reconstruction (1923) in both 'normal' and 'mirror' writing.

39

Menenstraat 14:
the Notebaert family

The Ypres family Notebaert – which ran
a leather goods and shoemaker's shop
here – was badly hit during the First
World War. On 6 and 7 November 1914,
father Joseph, son Albert and daughter
Gabrielle were all killed. Towards the
end of the war, the house on the corner
of Menenstraat and Harpestraat (also

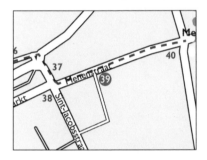

GODVRUCHTIG AANDENKEN VAN

Heer Josephus-Leopoldus-Petrus NOTEBAERT
Echtgenoot van Marie-Emiliana Verbeke,
geboren te Yper den 4 Juni 1850,
en zijne welbeminde kinders
Albertus-Josephus-Aloïsius-Cornelius
geboren te Yper den 4 Juni 1894,
en
Gabriella-Aloïsia-Eugenia-Cornelia
geboren te Yper den 15 Juli 1895,
te Yper als onschuldige slachtoffers van den oorlog
gestorven den 6 en 7 November 1914.

Above: Memento
of the three killed
members of the
Notebaert family,
November 1914.

Left: The approved
building design for
the reconstruction
of the shop and
home of widow
Notebaert and son,
3 May 1921.

Left: Bellewaerdestraat (now Harpestraat) shortly before the First World War. The house on the left was part of the property of the Notebaert family.

Below: Menenstraat near the corner with Grote Markt in 1918. (Australian War Memorial)

THE FATE OF THE LOCAL POPULATION DURING AND AFTER THE FIRST WORLD WAR

Between 4 August 1914 and 31 December 1918, at least 403 civilians died in the city of Ypres. It is certain, however, that there are many more. Due to the chaotic circumstances, many were not identified and remained in the rubble. Among these casualties are not only inhabitants of Ypres, but also refugees from elsewhere who sought asylum here. At least 700 inhabitants of Ypres lost their lives during the First World War, either in their hometown or elsewhere. That is almost one in twenty of the population of the inner city of Ypres at that time. After the war not all former inhabitants from Ypres returned. More than half of the pre-war population would resettle elsewhere.

known as Bellewaerdestraat) was completely razed to the ground. Widow Maria Verbeke and her remaining son returned to Ypres and reopened their shop in October 1920. By 1921 the building was rebuilt. The story of the Notebaert family, heavily battered from the war – where widow and son are confronted by great personal loss in a horrific war, only to be compounded the heavy administrative burden to obtain their war damage and rebuild their home – is that of many Ypres families.

A more winding Menenstraat in 1912.

40 The Menin Gate

After much wrangling over the preservation of part of the ruins on Grote Markt, the British settle with 'only' a memorial at the Menin Gate. This monumental hall is the most important British war memorial in Belgium. The walls are inscribed with the names of soldiers from the British Empire – those of India, Canada, Australia, among others – who lost their lives in the infamous Ypres Salient and who have no known grave. There are

Above: Louis Titz: *View of the Menin Gate at Ypres*, 1910. (Royal Collection of Belgium)

Right: The construction of the Menin Gate seen from Menenstraat, c.1925.

approximately 55,000 names here. Not all Commonwealth missing persons are commemorated here. For example, the New Zealanders have their own memorials to the missing close to the place where they died. For the dead of the United Kingdom (Great Britain and Ireland) the caesura lies on 15 August 1917: those who died afterwards are commemorated on the memorial to the missing in Tyne Cot Cemetery.

The Menin Gate – designed by Sir Reginald Blomfield (see no. 15) – is based on the classical triumphal arch and was solemnly unveiled in 1927. On the side of the town centre the gate is crowned by a shrouded cenotaph as if to remind the inhabitants of the town of the sacrifice of the British. Every evening at 8 p.m. – whether Christmas, or rain or snow or shine – the Last Post resounds here in honour of the casualties of the First World War.

While the Cloth Hall symbolises the reconstruction of Ypres after the First World War, the Menin Gate is the symbol of commemoration of the war dead.

Right: A snapshot from the audience at the unveiling of the Menin Gate, 24 July 1927.

Below: A Last Post ceremony, c.1930. Second from right is Pierre Vandenbraambussche, founder of the Last Post, fourth from the right is Henri Sobry, mayor of Ypres.